FUTURE TECH

COMMUNICATIONS
NOW AND INTO THE FUTURE

Steve Parker

ILLUSTRATED BY INDUSTRIAL ART STUDIO

Belitha Press

First published in Great Britain in 1998 by

 Belitha Press Limited
London House, Great Eastern Wharf
Parkgate Road, London SW11 4NQ

This edition first published in 1999

Series editor Veronica Ross
Editor Julie Hill
Designer Hayley Cove
Illustrations by Industrial Art Studio
Consultants Ian Graham and Virginia Whitby
Picture researcher Diana Morris

ISBN 1 85561 865 6 (paperback)
ISBN 1 85561 728 5 (hardback)

British Library Cataloguing in Publication Data
for this book is available from the British Library

Printed in China

Photo credits
Andrew Brookes/Getty Images: 13.
Miles Cort/Eye Ubiquitous: 27b.
Hayley Cove: 18b.
John Darling/Getty Images: 16.
Mary Kate Denny/Getty Images:5t.
C.M. Dixon: 6t, 6b.
Bruce Foster/Getty Images: 7b.
Getty Images: 2c. Pete Jones/Photofusion: 12.
Matthew McKee/Eye Ubiquitous: 7c.
Peter Menzell/SPL: 29.
Moviestore Collection: 8-9b.
Ian Murphy/Getty Images: 19.
NASA/SPL: 17. Greg Pease/Getty Images 5b.
Steven Peters/Getty Images: 23.
Peter Poulides/Getty Images: 10.
Ebet Roberts/Redferns: 21.
Paul Seheult/Eye Ubiquitous: 20.
Bob Thomason/Getty Images: 26-7.
Paul Thompson/Eye Ubiquitous: 8c.
Mark Wagner/Getty Images: 4.
Julia Waterlow/Eye Ubiquitous: 9t.
Randy Wells/Getty Images: 10-11.

Words in **bold** appear in the glossary on pages 30-31.

CONTENTS

INTRODUCTION

We spend at least one-third of our lives communicating. Communication means giving out and taking in information and knowledge. Almost every activity involves communication, such as listening to a teacher, talking to friends, reading a book, even watching television. By communicating we learn facts and figures, discover information, understand knowledge, develop our ideas and personalities, relate to other people and enjoy ourselves.

A pilot communicates with the crew, the on-board computer systems, air traffic control, and the passengers on the plane.

WHO OR WHAT COMMUNICATES?

Communication happens between people, when we talk face to face or send each other letters. People also communicate with each other through machines when they make phone calls, and send and receive **e-mails** and faxes. More and more, communication also happens between machines. Computers exchange huge amounts of information, or **data**, such as the latest prices in the world money markets, or the numbers of people buying a certain product.

TELECOMMUNICATIONS

This book looks at how we use science and technology to communicate. In particular, it looks at **telecommunications** – sending or receiving information over long distances. Telecommunications involves a range of machines, including telephones, radios, televisions, **fax machines**, **fibre-optic** cables, **microwave** links, **satellites**, **modems** and the **worldwide web** of computers known as the **Internet**. These are changing the way we learn, work, play and organize our daily lives.

> ## ▷ FUTURE TREND

Predicting the future is very difficult. A new invention may be in daily use in five years time, or it may be delayed for 30 years. It may never happen at all. What is certain is that technology develops all the time. Future Trend looks at new developments which may happen in 20, 40, or even 60 years. They may seem impossible to us today. But for people only 40 years ago, so was the Internet.

We learn by communicating with people, such as teachers, and with machines like computers.

▷ WHAT DO WE COMMUNICATE?

- Straightforward facts – what a famous scientist did, or the results of yesterday's big sports event.

- Thoughts and opinions – who is the best band in the music charts, or who is your favourite painter.

- Ideas and concepts – an idea for a new invention, or what an alien might look like.

- Plans – what are you doing this weekend?

Television control rooms are central parts of the global communications business.

EARLY COMMUNICATIONS

We are communicating with you, right now, in this book. Pictures and words were one of the earliest forms of communication. But before words and language, people relied on the sound of the human voice, facial expressions and gestures to communicate their thoughts, moods and intentions. This type of communication can only happen when people are near each other.

Before words came pictures. Cave paintings in many areas, including America, Europe and Australia, date back more than 20 000 years.

The first writing – lines, symbols and simple pictures in clay tablets – appeared about 5000 years ago.

SPEAKING AND WRITING

Language developed gradually in many places around the world. Speech evolved from the grunts made by early peoples into the kind of talking we do today in many different languages. Words made communication easier and more varied, with less chance of mistakes or confusion. People began to make written records by using symbols and letters.

BETTER COMMUNICATIONS

As civilizations developed, people began to communicate over distances. They used messengers to deliver handwritten documents by foot or on horseback. Better long-distance communication became important to carry out trade, build empires, control armies, and make expeditions of discovery across land and sea.

TOTAL COMS-IN-THE-WALL?
Most high streets have a hole-in-the-wall machine which gives you cash. One day this may be a TCM (total communications machine) with screen, keys, speakers, phone and printer. When you clip in your PIM (personal input module) and key in your PIN (personal identification number) you will be linked to the FutureNet for worldwide communication. You could watch TV, buy goods, talk on the phone, hear music...

TELECOMMUNICATIONS

'Tele' means at a distance, as in telecommunications or telecoms. The process of sending information fast over long distances happened in stages. It began with messengers and mail services carrying letters and parcels. These date back to ancient times. The first modern-style postal services for public use began in the 1400s in Europe, and soon spread to other regions. A breakthrough came in 1800 when the invention of the electricity-making battery made completely new forms of telecommunication possible. The invention of the telegraph, telephone, radio and television all relied on the power of electricity.

Mail offices sort thousands of letters every hour, using electronic machines to read the addresses – even those in wobbly handwriting.

> **FEW AND MANY**

Some communications are between limited numbers of people or they are one-to-one, such as talking on the telephone to a relative, or sending a letter to a friend. This is called personal communication. Mass

communication reaches many people – often millions – and is carried out through the media. The media include the print media of newspapers, books and magazines, the broadcast media of radio and television, and the electronic media of computers, e-mail and the Internet.

PAPER COMMUNICATIONS

One of the earliest and most important methods of communication was by words and pictures on paper. Paper communications take the personal form of letters, notes or packages, and the mass form of newspapers, magazines and books sold to millions of people. We like to read a daily newspaper, learn from an exciting information book (like this one), or curl up in bed with a good storybook.

Computers update a newspaper with the very latest information, before it is printed.

Every city has newsstands which sell magazines in dozens of different languages.

REACHING THE PUBLIC

The printing press was invented in the 1450s by German craftsman Johann Gutenberg. Before Gutenberg's time, every copy of a book was written and illustrated by hand. The invention of the printing press meant that thousands of copies could be produced by a machine. Mass printing made books cheaper and available to ordinary people. Printing changed education, as more people wanted to read, write, and learn about the world.

THE RISE OF PRINT

The first newspapers were printed in Germany and they spread through Europe in the 1500s. They began to carry information about certain items and products. This was the beginning of advertising. Today there are more than 60 000 daily or weekly newspapers around the world.

In the film *Tomorrow Never Dies*, James Bond battled a communications-controlling media mogul.

FACT OR FICTION?

Newspapers and magazines are a massive part of the global communications business. They influence our knowledge, beliefs and opinions. A story in a newspaper may be exactly that — a made-up story which is untrue. But it may be read and believed by millions of people. It could make or break a person's career, or create or ruin a business.

WILL PRINT DIE?

Some people believe that, one day, small computers will replace all books and newspapers. Yet more and more are printed each year. So why is the printed word still so popular?

- Newspapers, magazines and books cost very little, compared with a modern computer with its various programs and discs.

- They have no working parts to go wrong or batteries to run down.

- They can be picked up and put down quickly and easily, without the worry of opening computer programs or saving data.

DESKTOP PUBLISHING

Most books, magazines and newspapers are produced using **desktop publishing (DTP)** software on computers. The screen shows the pages as they will look when printed, with all the words and pictures in place. Changes can be made at the touch of a button. Before DTP, words and pictures were printed from wooden or metal blocks. A tiny change meant making a whole new block!

FUTURE TREND

LIVING NEWSPAPER?

Television shows news as it happens, anywhere in the world. But a big TV screen is bulky and needs electricity. A newspaper has large pictures and lots of words and folds away conveniently. But it contains yesterday's news. Could the two merge into the PNS – the portable news screen? Like a lightweight newspaper, it also has a large screen. It displays news in words and pictures, as it happens, sent direct from an international newsroom. It is constantly updated via its in-built aerial and solar-powered batteries. After use, you simply fold it away!

THE TELECOM NETWORK

Suppose you want to talk to a friend on the other side of the world. You pick up the phone, key in the number, wait for the answer and speak. It sounds simple. But making an international telephone call involves many stages and processes, using wires and cables, **radio waves** and microwaves, and high-tech equipment such as computers, **lasers** and satellites. Together, these make up the worldwide telecommunications **network**.

Within 30 years, telephone boxes and wires may disappear. Everyone could have a mobile phone.

LINKS IN THE SYSTEM

The telecom network uses many different technologies. Local phone lines to the nearby telephone exchange, especially in country areas, are usually metal wires carrying electrical signals. Bigger trunk cables or landlines between main exchanges are fibre-optic. The signals are strengthened at regular intervals by booster stations.

AROUND THE GLOBE

Long-distance calls can be sent along overground or undersea cables. Or they are beamed by a large dish antenna at a ground station up to a satellite in space. The satellite sends back the signals to a receiving dish thousands of kilometres away. Signals can also be beamed in stages over land or water by microwave links. These use small dish antennae on towers which are 30-50 kilometres apart.

1 A mobile phone changes your voice sounds into electrical signals, then into weak radio waves.

2 The waves are picked up by a transmitter-receiver (TR), part of the **cellular** network (see page 15).

Microwave dishes or antennae are on tall towers, on high hills, so the waves are not blocked.

3 The TR changes the radio signals back into electrical ones and sends them to the local exchange.

ALIENS CALLING?

Our communications equipment here on Earth works using radio waves. But radio waves are also produced naturally by objects in space, such as stars. A whole branch of science, called radio astronomy, is dedicated to observing them. Deep in space, maybe aliens are also using radio waves. As they explore the Universe, and our own radio-based communications improve, perhaps one day we could chat to them on mobile phones.

6 The satellite receives the signals, strengthens them, and beams them back down to another ground station two continents away.

5 The ground station changes the laser light signals to electrical ones and then to radio waves, which are beamed up to a **comsat** in space.

7 The signals are changed from radio waves into microwaves and beamed cross-country on a microwave link.

8 At the main exchange the microwaves become laser light signals again, for the fibre-optic network.

4 The local exchange converts electrical signals to flashes of laser light and sends these along fibre-optic cables.

9 After conversion from light to electricity at the local exchange, the signals reach the handset and become sounds again. Your voice comes out of the handset.

Modern communications is a very technical science. It brings together experts in engineering, electronics, light, sound and computers. Global telecommunications is based on the use of waves, such as radio and **light waves**. These travel so fast that they seem to cross continents in an instant. In fact they take about one-seventh of a second to go around the world. So live radio and television are not truly live!

LOTS OF WAVES

These waves are part of a whole range or spectrum of waves and rays, called the **electromagnetic spectrum** or EMS. All of these travel at the speed of light, 300 000 km per second. Only their size and numbers, or frequency, are different, as shown in the diagram.

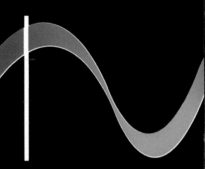

RADIO WAVES
Radio waves are used not only for radio, but also for television, and the radar of planes and ships.

MICROWAVES
Microwaves are used for cooking and for communications.

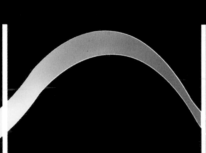

Waves can be varied, or modulated, either in height or numbers, giving AM and FM.

INFRA-RED WAVES
These have a heating effect. Very weak ones are used in TV and hi-fi remote controls.

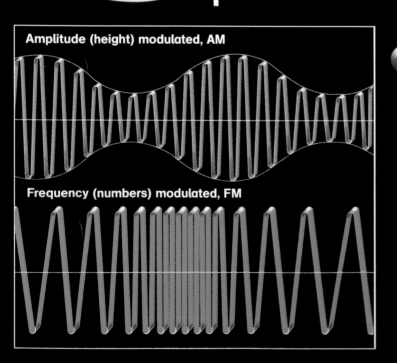

Amplitude (height) modulated, AM

Frequency (numbers) modulated, FM

FEATURES OF WAVES

The waves of the EMS have amplitude, wavelength and frequency. The amplitude is the tallness or height of the wave. The wavelength is the distance from a certain position on one wave to the same position on the next wave. The frequency is the number of waves going past a fixed point each second. This is measured in hertz (Hz).

INFO ON THE WAVES

So how are these waves used? Take a basic wave, called the carrier wave. Then vary it slightly. The variations follow a coded pattern that represents the information to be carried. In telecoms, the variations are called modulations. There are two main ways of varying or modulating a carrier wave (see diagram). One is to vary its height, or amplitude. This is known as AM or amplitude modulation. The other is to vary its frequency. This is called frequency modulation or FM.

MORE WAVES, MORE INFO

Radio wavelengths vary from one metre to many kilometres. Light waves are much shorter, with millions in one centimetre. More waves per second gives more waves to change, or modulate. This increases the information which can be carried. Fibre-optics uses laser light as the carrier wave. One fibre-optic can carry as much information as 10 000 telephone wires. This is why fibre-optic cables, containing thousands of individual fibres, are used in the telecommunications network.

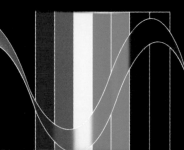

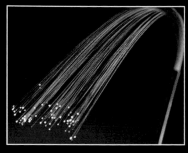

ULTRA-VIOLET WAVES
Ultra-violet waves are used for killing germs and sterilizing food and medical equipment.

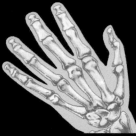

GAMMA RAYS
Gamma rays are used in **radiation** for the breaking up of **atoms**.

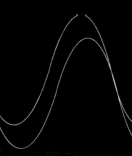

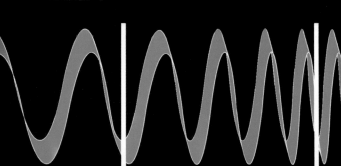

LIGHT WAVES
Light waves are the ones we can see with our eyes. They vary in colour from red, through green, to violet.

X RAYS
These waves have lots of energy and can be dangerous. They are used for seeing into the body and for destroying diseased parts such as cancer growths.

▶ FUTURE TREND

SELF DESTRUCTION?
Modern armed forces use communications which are so advanced and secret, we do not know about them. There are spy satellites, planes and subs which keep watch on boats, aircraft and vehicles. Whoever controls the communications has the upper hand. An evil dictator could win a war without any weapons. Simply interfere with, or jam, the enemy's communications, then send signals telling the enemy's weapons to attack themselves.

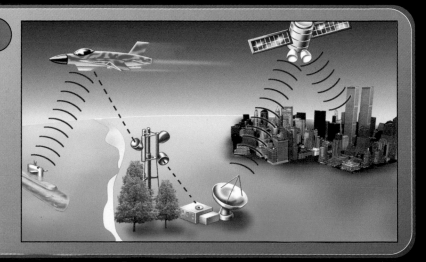

TELEPHONE TECH

The telephone handset has changed little in almost 100 years. The sound waves of your voice change into electrical signals. These travel along the curly connecting cord, through the base set, and along the phone line into the telecom system. Electrical signals also travel the other way, to the earpiece of the receiving telephone, where they are turned into sound waves for your ear.

diaphragm

carbon grains

1 The caller speaks into the microphone of the mouthpiece.

2 The microphone has a thin sheet or diaphragm at the front. When you speak, the diaphragm vibrates in time with the sound waves of your voice.

3 The moving diaphragm squashes grains of carbon behind it, which have a small current of electricity passing through them. This varies the amount of electricity.

0144 317690

WAVES TO NUMBERS

Many older parts of the telecom network use **analogue** technology. This means they turn sound waves into similar waves of electrical signals, which vary in strength. But gradually, the network is being changed to **digital** technology. This means the sound waves are converted into strings of digits — the binary numbers 0 and 1.

▷ FUTURE TREND

VIDEOPHONE ON THE WRIST?
Wristwatch televisions already exist.
A future development might be the wristwatch **videophone**. It would have a small screen and camera, and a small microphone and speaker, plus tiny buttons for keying in the numbers. Then you could see and hear the person at the other end of the line. You would also be seen and heard. If it was waterproof, you could even use it in the bath …

THE MOBILE

A mobile phone is like a standard telephone with a low-power radio transmitter-receiver. The sound waves of your voice are converted into electrical signals and then into **radio signals** which the phone transmits from its aerial. These are picked up by one of the network's transmitter-receivers, usually on a nearby tower. The phone also receives radio signals from the transmitter-receiver, and converts them into electrical signals, and then into sound waves for the earpiece.

CELLULAR NETWORKS

Mobile phones are small and light because their radio signals are low-powered and they rely on a cellular network. A country is divided into a patchwork of cells. Each cell is an area a few kilometres across, with a transmitter-receiver near its centre. The phone is never more than a few kilometres away from a transmitter-receiver, and locks on to the signals from the nearest. If the user is moving, the phone switches between transmitter-receivers as it moves from cell to cell.

4 The wave-like variations in the electrical signals from the mouthpiece copy the variations in the sounds of your voice. This way of coding information is called analogue.

5 An electronic device, a modem (see page 23) measures the analogue wave heights every split second.

6 The measurements are changed into strings of on-off pulses which are bits (binary digits) for the digital network.

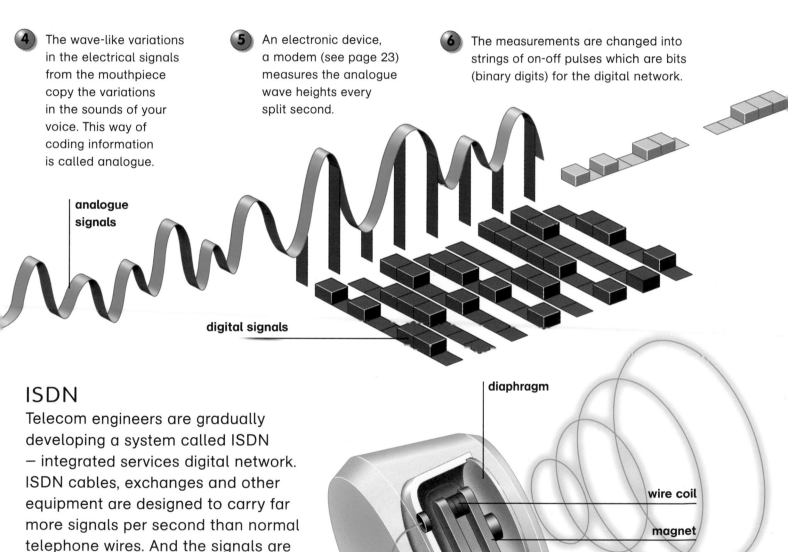

analogue signals

digital signals

diaphragm

wire coil

magnet

ISDN

Telecom engineers are gradually developing a system called ISDN — integrated services digital network. ISDN cables, exchanges and other equipment are designed to carry far more signals per second than normal telephone wires. And the signals are all digital, rather than a mixture of analogue and digital. This means you can connect a telephone, computer, video camera, loudspeaker, microphone and fax machine to one ISDN line, and use them all at the same time!

7 Digital signals must be changed back into analogue form, as electrical waves, to make the earpiece produce sounds.

RADIO CENTRAL

As television has become more widespread, so radio has become less important in daily life. But listening to the radio is still popular, especially while doing something else. Because radio is sound alone, it allows the eyes and mind to concentrate elsewhere. People can listen while driving, rollerblading or windsurfing, working on routine jobs in an office or factory – even doing homework!

Emergency radio uses special frequencies which normal sets cannot receive.

USING YOUR IMAGINATION

Listening to the radio also exercises your imagination. When you listen to a play on the radio, you have to picture the characters and scenery, rather than being shown them on-screen. And radio is ideal for music, which is such a popular part of daily life. You can catch up with the charts, and close your eyes as you listen, to create images in your mind...

NOT JUST RADIO

Radio waves are not used just to broadcast radio programmes. They carry television programmes and they are an important part of the telecom network, carrying signals across land and sea, to satellites and space stations. Some radio frequencies are kept for emergency radio beacons and services such as police, fire, ambulance and coastguard.

▷ AM AND FM

We identify radio stations by their names, band groups, and frequencies. The two main band groups are AM and FM (as explained on page 13). The frequency is shown on the tuning dial or display. For FM stations it is measured in megahertz, MHz. For example, a radio station called Hundred FM might broadcast at 100 MHz. This means it sends out 100 million radio waves each second.

In general, FM gives higher quality sound than AM, and in stereo. It is also less prone to interference by bad weather. But it may not have such a great range, fading more quickly than AM as you travel further away from the transmitter.

RADIO GRIDLOCK?

Radio waves are used for radio and TV and for making phone calls. As these waves increase in number and power, could they cause problems? One day, there might be so many that they interfere with each other, jam broadcasts, and wipe out radio links. The result would be worldwide chaos. To prevent this, we might have to wait in a queuing system before making a phone call or logging on to the Internet. So much for progress!

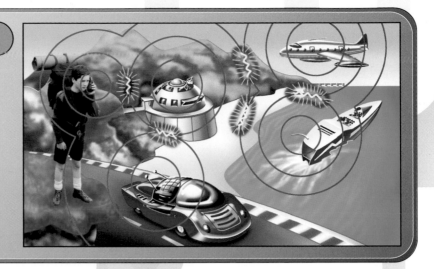

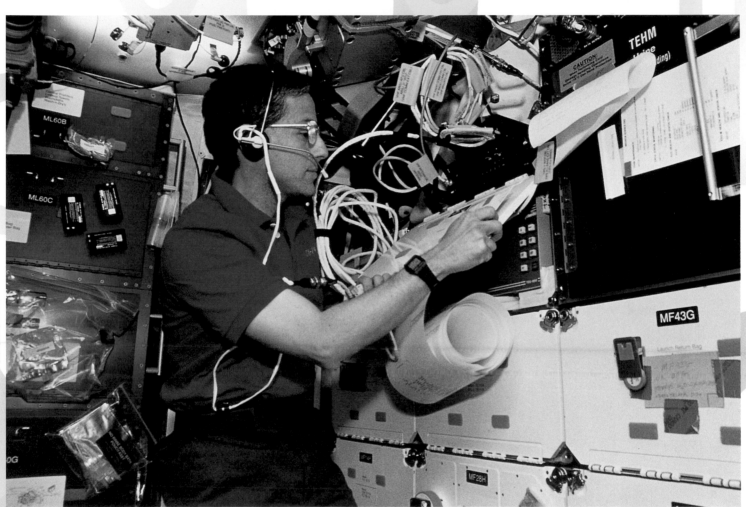

Radio is the only link between spaceships and Earth. It is used for talking and TV pictures as well as for navigating and swapping computer information.

MORE RADIO USES

Radio waves are used in many kinds of specialized scientific and work communications. Ships, planes and vehicles use radio to communicate with each other and their control bases. Mobile and cordless phones, walkie-talkies and CB (citizen's band) also depend on radio waves. So do radar and satellite navigation systems, weather satellites, and the tracking bugs that are fixed to boats, planes, people, and even animals, such as whales, which travel over long distances.

TV GALORE

 How long do you spend watching television each day? If you gave a truthful answer, you might be surprised or even worried! Television is today's main method of mass communication. We learn from it through wildlife and history programmes. We keep up to date with news and current affairs through news programmes and documentaries. And we watch drama and comedy programmes for amusement and entertainment.

TYPES OF TELEVISION

A television programme can reach a television set in several ways. These include:

SATELLITE
The usual system is DBS: direct broadcast by satellite. The programme is received by and beamed back to Earth from a satellite as specially-coded radio waves (see page 27). A dish-shaped antenna detects the waves, and a decoder feeds them into an ordinary TV set.

(see page 27)

TERRESTRIAL BROADCAST
Programmes are sent out, or broadcast, in the form of radio waves, from antennae (aerials) on tall towers or masts. In most countries there is a network of these towers or masts dotted across the land. But the radio waves may be blocked or distorted by mountains, tall buildings or bad weather.

VIDEO
A video can record television programmes on magnetic tape, which can be played back and watched later. A video machine is usually near the TV set. But if it is linked by high-capacity cables through the telecom network, it could be in the next street, or town, or even in another country.

CABLE
A **cable**, usually a fibre-optic bundle buried in the ground, carries the programme directly into a home or building. Cable TV is available in many cities and towns, but it is less common in country areas, where houses are further apart. Signals can be sent the other way along the cable, from house to broadcaster, allowing two-way communication.

DIGITAL TV

Most television broadcasts use analogue radio waves (see page 14). From the late 1990s, broadcasters began to make both satellite and **terrestrial broadcasts** using digital radio waves. This means clearer, better pictures and sound, and far more choice. Between five and ten digital channels can be broadcast in place of one analogue channel.

A TV studio is packed with cameras, microphones and other high-tech communications equipment.

CHANNEL CHOICE

Hundreds of channels will show more programmes and more choices for each programme. One show could use up to ten channels. Each one would show the viewpoint of a different camera, or show a different commentator, talking in the language of your choice.

▷ FUTURE TREND

JUST LIKE BEING THERE?
If you attend a big event, you can walk around and look at what you want. On ordinary television, you have to watch the single scene that broadcasters decide to show. The future's MCTV (multi-channel television) gives you far more choice. A sports event might take up 40 channels. On your multi-screen you could select your own scenes, the camera angles for them and your preferred reporters. Even better than being there?

Communications use lots of screens. Almost every office, factory, school and home has at least one screen. From them we get information in visual form through TV sets, computer monitors, closed-circuit TV systems and video recordings.

Hand-sized TV sets show a bright, clear picture. But they tend to use up batteries quickly.

TELEVISION AND COMPUTER SCREENS

The standard screen for a television or computer uses scanning beam technology. The screen is the front part of a large glass container called a tube. This has no air inside – it is a vacuum. The narrow end of the tube has three **electron** guns. These fire streams of tiny particles, called electrons. Focusing plates bend the beams, so that each one traces a line across the top of the screen, then a line just below it, and so on, line by line down the screen.

1. Electron guns fire streams of electron particles. These are invisible so they have no colour.

2. Focusing plates, charged with static electricity, make the beams bend so each scans the screen 25 times every second.

3. The beam from each gun is angled to pass through a hole in a mask, so that it strikes only one colour of dot on the screen.

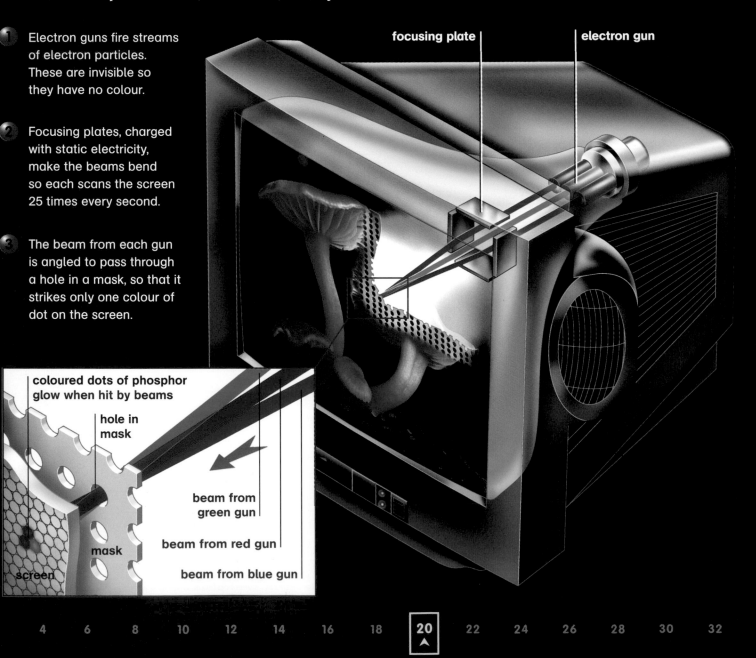

focusing plate

electron gun

coloured dots of phosphor glow when hit by beams

hole in mask

beam from green gun

beam from red gun

mask

beam from blue gun

screen

TYPES OF TV SET

TV sets range from pocket versions to giant screens bigger than a house, like those at sports events and concerts. Home cinema has a set with a large, wide screen, and surround-sound loudspeakers to increase the spectacular effect of images and sounds. **High-definition television (HDTV)** has a large, wide screen which gives a clearer picture.

Even at the back of a huge crowd, you can feel close to the action if there's a giant viewscreen.

NEW-GENERATION SCREENS

Standard scanning-beam screens are heavy, bulky and use lots of electricity. Newer screens are lightweight and flat, like a picture hung on a wall. Yet they give brighter pictures and use less electricity. Some are based on liquid-crystal technology. These screens can be moved about as they are linked to the TV set or computer by an infra-red beam.

▶ FUTURE TREND

3D IN THIN AIR?

Flat and wide screens will come, and probably go. The next stage may be TV with pictures in three dimensions and no screen. Instead, a small box containing a hologram projector will shine laser beams into the air, to make moving, 3D colour images that you can walk round. You could view a whole sports stadium in miniature, watch the action from any viewpoint and cheer on your favourite team – all in the privacy of your own bedroom.

COMPUTER-COM

 A computer has many different parts. To work properly, these parts need to communicate with each other. They do so using a language of tiny pulses of electricity – millions each second. These represent the 0s and 1s of digital code. The coded pulses can represent any form of information — words, symbols, photographs, diagrams, moving pictures, speech or music.

LOCAL NETWORKS

A computer can communicate directly with another computer by sending and receiving tiny pulses of electricity along a cable. Computers can also communicate directly with other electronic devices that use digital technology, such as fax machines, **digi-cameras**, digital telephones and image scanners. These machines may be linked together in an office, factory or group of buildings to form a local area network, or LAN. This is like a small, private telecom system, and it's totally digital.

 NETWORK

Computers and similar devices can be linked into a ring network. Signals go out of a machine along its device spur, around the ring, and into the correct destination device.

fax machine

device spur

ring network

telephone

computer

device spur

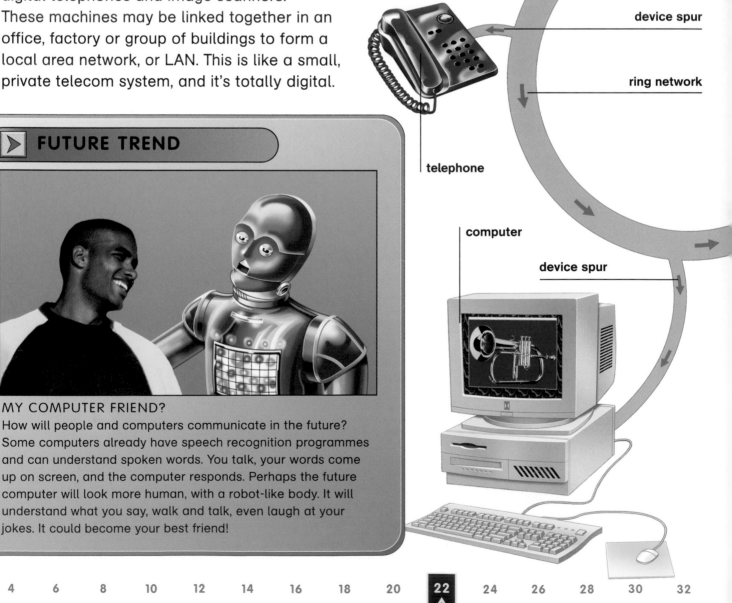

▷ FUTURE TREND

MY COMPUTER FRIEND?
How will people and computers communicate in the future? Some computers already have speech recognition programmes and can understand spoken words. You talk, your words come up on screen, and the computer responds. Perhaps the future computer will look more human, with a robot-like body. It will understand what you say, walk and talk, even laugh at your jokes. It could become your best friend!

THE MODEM

Sending digital signals direct from a computer into the global telecom network would cause problems. This is because the older, analogue parts of the network cannot deal with them. So most computers use a special electronic device called a modem (see page 15). This converts the digital signals used by computers into analogue signals that can travel through the telephone network. At the other end, another modem changes the analogue signals back into digital ones. Gradually, as the worldwide telecom system becomes digital, modems will no longer be needed.

computer

device spur

01101100011001011

digital signals

modem

The user of the computer on page 22 sends the image of a musical instrument to a friend overseas (see page 25).

link to main telecom and worldwide web

analogue signals

LIMITS ON THE LINES

The older, analogue parts of the telecom system can carry only a limited number of signals, at limited speeds. This is one reason why a videophone produces a small, unclear picture. Standard phone lines cannot carry the huge number of signals at the rapid rate needed to build up a large, sharp, detailed, coloured moving image on a videophone.

LIFELIKE PICTURES

Modern phone lines, especially fibre-optic and ISDN lines, are high-capacity – they can carry more signals at greater speeds in digital form. This means they can carry clear, full-colour and detailed moving images, such as cinema films or videophone pictures, plus hi-fi quality sound, into a computer or television set.

People in different places can see and hear each other at a video conference.

The Internet is an international network of computers and similar electronic machines, linked by the wires, cables, radio waves and satellites of the telecom system. The system converts and carries signals between computers in the same way that it carries the sounds of a telephone call.

FASTER AND BIGGER

The Internet is growing fast – millions more people use it every year. The Net forms a vast, web-like system around the world, through which computers can exchange information at high speed. For example, all the words in this book could be sent anywhere in the world in less than a minute. Information exchanged on the Net can be in the form of words, pictures, diagrams, sounds — anything a computer can handle.

▷ THE WORLDWIDE WEB

Many parts of the Internet are used for private communication. Other parts, such as the worldwide web, make millions of pages of information available to millions of people. This information is provided by governments, businesses, universities, libraries, advertisers, sales teams, special interest groups, and almost any other kind of group or person.

A regional hub (purple circle) is the exchange for a number of metropolitan hubs. It covers a large part of a state or country.

Information can come into a region as radio waves from a satellite or microwaves on a cross-country link.

Each end-user (red square) has a two-way link with a metropolitan hub. The end-user in the blue house is buying something from a shopping mall abroad at the other end of the yellow pathway. End-users can be homes, schools, farms, factories or other buildings.

A metropolitan hub (blue hexagon) is the central exchange for all the houses, offices, factories and other buildings in an area, such as a city, town or group of villages.

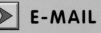

FUTURE TREND

SPACENET?

The Internet is spreading all over the globe. If space travel becomes common, the Net might extend to orbiting space stations, deep-space probes, and manned bases on the Moon and nearby planets. But communication could be slow. It can take up to 40 minutes for laser or radio waves to travel from Earth to Mars and back. If you ask a question, that's a long pause until the answer arrives! Unless we discover waves that travel faster than light...

THE COMPUTER'S JOBS

For the Internet, a computer is needed to store information you want to send, or information it has received. Special programs in the computer process the information. Programs called **search engines** scan the Internet or worldwide web, looking for the key words or symbols you have fed into the computer. You might use a search engine if you wanted to find out about a topic, such as sharks, but didn't know which web sites were about sharks. Web browsers help you to navigate, or find your way around.

E-MAIL

E-mail, or electronic mail, does much the same as ordinary mail. You can send letters, documents and other information by e-mail. The sender and receiver must have computers connected to the telecom network. Your computer sends your e-mail to a central electronic postbox. It can be sent on to the receiver at once, or later, when convenient. The whole process takes seconds. A letter in the postal system takes much longer, one or a few days. Supporters of e-mail call the ordinary postal system 'snail-mail'.

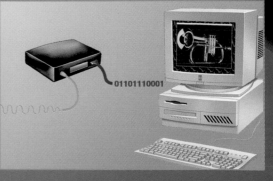

01101110001

In a skyscraper on the other side of the world, the computer-user's friend receives the image sent via the Internet (pages 22-23).

SATELLITE COMS

More than 2000 satellites are orbiting the Earth and more than 500 of them are involved in telecommunications. The main ones are known as comsats or communications satellites. They send and receive radio and microwave signals from satellite ground stations on the Earth's surface.

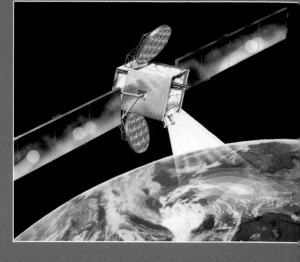

THE EARTH IN THE WAY

Most radio signals cannot be sent directly between ground stations, because, like light waves, radio waves travel in straight lines. Over such long distances, the curve of the Earth's surface is in the way, and the waves beam straight into space.

A comsat beams its radio waves down over a certain area, called its footprint.

GETTING AROUND THE PROBLEM

A typical comsat has a special type of orbit: **geostationary orbit (GEO)**, 35 787 kilometres directly above the Equator. At this distance, the satellite takes exactly 24 hours to go once round the Earth. The Earth also spins once every 24 hours. This means that, when seen from the Earth, the satellite seems to stay in the same place all the time.

▷ FUTURE TREND

NEVER LOST AGAIN?

The GPS (global positioning system) is a worldwide system for pinpointing your location. It relies on a network of satellites sending out signals which are analyzed by a hand-held receiver. In the future, GPS receivers could be as small as microchips, and they could transmit signals to satellites. Fix one to your pet's collar, and you could track it down in moments!

GROUND STATIONS

GEO means that signals can be beamed from dish-shaped antenna at a ground station on Earth, always in the same direction, straight up to the satellite. With other types of orbit the dish would have to track the satellite across the sky. For part of the time, the satellite would be out of range, on the other side of the planet. GEO also means that the satellite can aim its signals down to its receiving ground station.

UPLINK AND DOWNLINK

Comsats receive radio signals from one ground station on the **uplink**. The satellite strengthens them, and beams them back on the **downlink** to another ground station, thousands of kilometres away. The radio signals represent all kinds of coded information, from phone calls and TV programmes to computer data for business, the military, e-mail and the Internet. A modern comsat can handle 30 000 phone calls and five television channels at the same time.

Huge dish antennae pick up not only our own radio signals, but also those coming naturally from deep space.

Live TV coverage of a major world event, such as the Olympic Games, may involve three or four satellite links.

▷ SATELLITE TV

Downlink signals are aimed at a dish aerial, 18 metres or more across, at a ground station. For television programmes, the signals are then broadcast through the terrestrial network. Satellite television signals also come from satellites in GEO, but go direct to our homes. This is called direct broadcast by satellite. DBS signals must be very powerful, so they can spread over a wide area, and be received by small domestic dish aerials.

COMMUNICATION OVERLOAD!

We are in the middle of an information revolution. This is a revolution in the the way we receive or send more knowledge and information, about more topics and subjects, more quickly, to more people and more places, all around the world. The information revolution is based on the vast, complicated and global business of telecommunications. But where is it taking us?

THE PC MACHINE

If you line up a mobile phone, pager, satellite navigation receiver, personal stereo, pocket television, mini-printer and the latest palmtop computer, they all look similar in size and shape, and fit neatly in the hand. One day, perhaps all these devices will be combined into one, the personal communicator, with a constant radio link to the Internet. With this, you could access any kind of personal or mass communication and get information, anywhere, at any time. You could see and talk to whoever you want, find out your exact location, choose from thousands of TV channels, print out pages, even play computer games — by yourself, or with anyone else anywhere in the world!

▷ FUTURE TREND

TOTAL COMMUNICATION
The personal communicator of the future may not be a hand-held device, but would hover in the air alongside you wherever you went. It would have no keyboard — you would speak your instructions. The batteries would be continually recharged by light or movement. In this way the personal communicator could be hands-off and wire-free, and would link you directly with 3D vision and stereo sound into the global telecom network.

DULL FUTURE?

What would we do if any piece of information or person was available instantly? There would be no challenge in finding information, and no excitement when you succeed in discovering it. Why would we bother to learn anything at all, if we could summon it at the press of a button or a word of instruction?

These people are wearing headsets to experience the sights and sounds of virtual reality.

STAY AT HOME?

There would be no need for travel and holidays – we would hardly ever go anywhere. Not only facts and knowledge, but also our relatives and friends, even the whole world, could come to us. We would live tele-lives, with tele-school, tele-work, tele-entertainment, tele-partying.

ANOTHER VIEW

On the other hand, this vision of the future might be fun. We could find out anything we wanted. This would give us lots more free time, without being stuck in classrooms, cars, buses and trains. We could make new friends around the globe, see and hear exotic places, and one day, perhaps even smell and taste any kind of food and drink. The information revolution would be complete. But what then?

GLOSSARY

analogue A way of coding information that uses waves which vary continuously in their height (amplitude) or number (frequency).

atoms Tiny particles – too small to be seen – that make up all objects and matter, including our bodies.

cable In television, usually a bundle of fibre-optics which can carry huge numbers of signals, as flashes of laser light – enough for full-colour TV pictures.

cellular Divided into separate parts or units called cells, like a bee's honeycomb, the rooms (cells) in a prison or the microscopic cells in a living thing.

citizen's band A range of radio frequencies that any citizen (anyone) can use for communication.

comsat A communications satellite, which receives signals from one area of Earth and sends them on to other places.

data Information of any kind, such as facts, figures, letters, numbers, words and symbols, including information such as pictures and sounds in coded form.

desktop publishing (DTP) Preparing something for publishing and printing, such as a newspaper, book or magazine, using computers which fit on a desktop.

digi-camera A camera which records a picture in digital form, as codes of numbers, rather than as an image on photographic film.

digital A way of coding information that uses series or strings of numbers (digits) – usually only two, 0 and 1, which are called binary digits or bits.

downlink The radio or microwave signals coming from a satellite down to Earth.

e-mail Electronic mail – letters, messages or notes sent by computer through the telecom network, in electronic form, rather than as marks on paper.

electromagnetic spectrum (EMS) A range of rays which are types of energy that travel like waves. They differ in the size of their wavelengths. The spectrum includes radio waves, microwaves, infra-red waves, light waves, ultra-violet rays, x-rays and gamma rays.

electron One of the basic particles of matter in the Universe. Atoms are made of electrons and other basic particles.

fax machine A machine which sends and receives documents on paper, using the telephone system.

fibre-optic A thin, hair-like strand, or fibre, made up of clear glass or plastic, which carries pulses of light along its length. Optics is the science of light.

gamma rays Rays or waves which are part of the electromagnetic spectrum (EMS). They are similar to light and x-rays, but have shorter waves. They are made by nuclear reactions and radioactive substances, and also come from space.

geostationary orbit (GEO) A satellite orbit around the Earth where the satellite seems to hang or hover in the same place all the time, when seen from Earth's surface. Satellites in other orbits seem to move across the sky.

high-definition television (HDTV) A television with a larger screen than a normal TV, and also more coloured dots packed into each tiny area, which give a clearer, sharper, more detailed and more colourful picture.

infra-red Rays or waves which are part of the electromagnetic spectrum (EMS). They are similar to visible light rays, but have waves slightly longer than those of visible red light. We cannot see infra-red rays, but we can feel them as they can have a warming or heating effect.

interference Changing, or distorting or altering in some way, usually for the worse.

Internet The worldwide network or web of computers and similar electronic machines, linked by the wires, cables and satellites of the telephone system.

laser A device which produces a narrow, very bright beam of light. Laser light is one pure colour and all its waves are exactly the same length. It can carry phone calls, play CDs and read information on CD-ROMs. Lasers are used for telecommunications and in many other ways.

light waves Waves or rays which are part of the electromagnetic spectrum (EMS). Light rays can be detected by our eyes. The rays range in colour from red through green to blue and violet, the colours of the light spectrum.

microwaves Rays or waves which are part of the electromagnetic spectrum (EMS). They are similar to radio and light rays, and the waves are about 1 to 100 centimetres long. We cannot see them, but we can use them to make heat

modem A machine that changes digital signals (made up of the binary digits 0 and 1) from a computer into signals that are suitable for the telephone system, or vice versa (back again).

network A number of machines linked together and communicating with each other.

radiation Any form of energy that is given out, or radiated, from a source as rays, waves or particles.

radio signals Radio waves of varying strengths, or in on-off pulses, which carry information in coded form. The information can include words, pictures, sounds and computer data.

radio waves Rays or waves which are part of the electromagnetic spectrum (EMS). They are similar to microwaves and light rays, but their waves are much longer, from one metre to many kilometres.

rays A form of energy that can be sent out as beams or waves.

satellite Something which goes around, or orbits, something else. For example, the Earth is a satellite of the Sun. The term is usually used for man-made objects travelling around the Earth.

search engine A computer program that searches or scans all the information available to it, usually through the telecom network, looking for key (important) words, letters or symbols.

terrestrial broadcast Radio or similar waves sent out from masts or towers on the ground, rather than from planes high in the sky or satellites in space.

telecommunications Sending, receiving, or communicating information over long distances, such as between computers or telephones. Telecommunications systems use metal wires, fibre-optic cables, radio signals, satellite links and other methods.

ultra-violet Rays or waves which are part of the electromagnetic spectrum (EMS). They are similar to light rays, but their waves are shorter. We cannot see ultra-violet rays, but they are responsible for tanning our skins in sunshine. Too much ultra-violet light can be harmful and cause burning.

uplink The radio or microwave signals going from Earth up to a satellite in space.

videophone A telephone on which you can see, as well as hear, the other person.

worldwide web Millions of electronic pages of information available through the Internet for public use — though sometimes at a price.

x-rays Rays or waves which are part of the electromagnetic spectrum (EMS). They are similar to radio and light rays, but their waves are very short, with millions packed into one centimetre. They can pass through soft substances such as flesh and wood, but not through dense substances such as bone and many metals. X-rays can harm living things, even in small amounts.

INDEX